To:

From:

Message:

Published by Christian Art Publishers

PO Box 1599, Vereeniging, 1930, RSA

© 2018

First edition 2018

Designed by Christian Art Publishers

Images used under license from Shutterstock.com

Illustrations used are in the public domain

Scripture quotations are taken from the *Holy Bible*, New Living Translation®, copyright © 1996, 2004, 2007, 2013, 2015 by Tyndale House Foundation. Used by permission of Tyndale House Publishers, Inc., Carol Stream, Illinois 60188. All rights reserved.

Scripture quotations are taken from the New King James Version. Copyright © 1979, 1980, 1982 by Thomas Nelson, Inc. Used by permission. All rights reserved.

Scripture quotations are taken from the *Holy Bible,* New International Version® NIV®. Copyright © 1973, 1978, 1984, 2011 by International Bible Society. Used by permission of Biblica, Inc.® All rights reserved worldwide.

Scripture quotations are taken from the *Holy Bible*, English Standard Version. Copyright © 2001 by Crossway Bibles, a publishing ministry of Good News Publishers. Used by permission. All rights reserved.

Scripture quotations are taken from the *Holy Bible*, Contemporary English Version®. Copyright © 1995 by American Bible Society. All rights reserved.

Printed in China

ISBN 978-1-4321-2911-8

18 19 20 21 22 23 24 25 26 27 – 10 9 8 7 6 5 4 3 2 1

PRAYERS

& Praises

from the Word

**CHRISTIAN ART
PUBLISHERS**

The Lord's Prayer

Our Father in heaven,
may Your name be kept holy.
May Your Kingdom come soon.
May Your will be done on earth,
as it is in heaven.
Give us today the food we need,
and forgive us our sins,
as we have forgiven those who sin against us.
And don't let us yield to temptation,
but rescue us from the evil one.

MATTHEW 6:9-13

I Will Praise You

I will praise You with my whole heart;
before the gods I will sing praises to You.
I will worship toward Your holy temple,
and praise Your name
for Your lovingkindness and Your truth;
for You have magnified Your word above all Your name.
In the day when I cried out, You answered me,
and made me bold with strength in my soul.
All the kings of the earth shall praise You, O LORD,
when they hear the words of Your mouth.
Yes, they shall sing of the ways of the LORD,
for great is the glory of the LORD.

PSALM 138:1-5

I Seek the Lord

O God, You are my God; earnestly I seek You;
my soul thirsts for You;
my flesh faints for You,
as in a dry and weary land where there is no water.
So I have looked upon You in the sanctuary,
beholding Your power and glory.
Because Your steadfast love is better than life,
my lips will praise You.

PSALM 63:1-3

You Make Me Strong

My heart rejoices in the LORD!
The LORD has made me strong.
Now I have an answer for my enemies;
I rejoice because You rescued me.
No one is holy like the LORD!
There is no one besides You;
there is no Rock like our God.

1 SAMUEL 2:1-2

Over All Things

O Lord, the God of our ancestor Israel,
may You be praised forever and ever!
Yours, O Lord, is the greatness, the power,
the glory, the victory, and the majesty.
Everything in the heavens and on earth is Yours,
O Lord, and this is Your kingdom.
We adore You as the One who is over all things.
Wealth and honor come from You alone,
for You rule over everything.
Power and might are in Your hand,
and at Your discretion
people are made great and given strength.

1 CHRONICLES 29:10-12

I Entrust
My Life to You

Show me the way I should go,

for to You I entrust my life.

Teach me to do Your will,

for You are my God;

may Your good Spirit

lead me on level ground.

For Your name's sake, LORD, preserve my life;

in Your righteousness, bring me out of trouble.

PSALM 143:8, 10-11

You Are My Help

I lift up my eyes to the hills.
From where does my help come?
My help comes from the LORD,
who made heaven and earth.
He will not let your foot be moved;
He who keeps you will not slumber.
Behold, He who keeps Israel
will neither slumber nor sleep.
The LORD is your keeper;
the LORD is your shade on your right hand.
The sun shall not strike you by day,
nor the moon by night.
The LORD will keep you from all evil;
He will keep your life.
The LORD will keep
your going out and your coming in
from this time forth and forevermore.

PSALM 121

Save Me from the Storm

Be merciful to me, O God, be merciful to me,
for in You my soul takes refuge;
in the shadow of Your wings I will take refuge,
till the storms of destruction pass by.
I cry out to God Most High,
to God who fulfills His purpose for me.
He will send from heaven and save me.
God will send out His steadfast love
and His faithfulness!

PSALM 57:1-3

I Love You, Lord

I love You, LORD, my strength.
The LORD is my rock, my fortress and my deliverer;
my God is my rock, in whom I take refuge,
my shield and the horn of my salvation, my stronghold.
I called to the LORD, who is worthy of praise,
and I have been saved.
He reached down from on high and took hold of me;
He drew me out of deep waters.
He brought me out into a spacious place;
He rescued me because He delighted in me.

PSALM 18:1-3, 16, 19

The Prayer of Jacob

O God of my grandfather Abraham, and God of my father, Isaac—O Lord, You told me, "Return to your own land and to your relatives." And You promised me, "I will treat you kindly." I am not worthy of all the unfailing love and faithfulness You have shown to me, Your servant. When I left home and crossed the Jordan River, I owned nothing except a walking stick. Now my household fills two large camps! O Lord, please rescue me from the hand of my brother, Esau. I am afraid that he is coming to attack me, along with my wives and children. But You promised me, "I will surely treat you kindly, and I will multiply your descendants until they become as numerous as the sands along the seashore—too many to count."

GENESIS 32:9-12

You Are My Rock

*I*n You, O LORD, do I take refuge;
let me never be put to shame!
In Your righteousness deliver me and rescue me;
incline Your ear to me, and save me!
Be to me a rock of refuge,
to which I may continually come;
You have given the command to save me,
for You are my rock and my fortress.
You, O LORD, are my hope,
my trust, O LORD, from my youth.

PSALM 71:1-3, 5

Forgive Our Rebellion

*L*ord, the great and awesome God,
who keeps His covenant of love
with those who love Him
and keep His commandments,
we have sinned and done wrong.
We have been wicked and have rebelled;
we have turned away from Your commands and laws.
LORD, You are righteous,
but this day we are covered with shame.
The Lord our God is merciful and forgiving,
even though we have rebelled against Him.

DANIEL 9:4-5, 7, 9

Tread Our Sins Underfoot

*W*ho is a God like You,
who pardons sin and forgives the transgression
of the remnant of His inheritance?
You do not stay angry forever
but delight to show mercy.
You will again have compassion on us;
You will tread our sins underfoot
and hurl all our iniquities into the depths of the sea.

MICAH 7:18-19

Thank You, Lord

It is good to give thanks to the LORD,
to sing praises to the Most High.
It is good to proclaim
Your unfailing love in the morning,
Your faithfulness in the evening.
You thrill me, LORD, with all You have done for me!
I sing for joy because of what You have done.
O LORD, what great works You do!
And how deep are Your thoughts.

PSALM 92:1-2, 4-5

We Recount Your Wondrous Deeds

We give thanks to You, O God;
we give thanks, for Your name is near.
We recount Your wondrous deeds.
I will declare it forever;
I will sing praise to the God of Jacob.

PSALM 75:1, 9

You Know Me Best

*Y*ou have searched me, LORD,
and You know me.
You know when I sit and when I rise;
You perceive my thoughts from afar.
You discern my going out and my lying down;
You are familiar with all my ways.
Before a word is on my tongue
You, LORD, know it completely.
Where can I go from Your Spirit?
Where can I flee from Your presence?
If I go up to the heavens, You are there;
if I make my bed in the depths, You are there.
If I rise on the wings of the dawn,
if I settle on the far side of the sea,
even there Your hand will guide me,
Your right hand will hold me fast.
Search me, God, and know my heart;
test me and know my anxious thoughts.
See if there is any offensive way in me,
and lead me in the way everlasting.

PSALM 139:1-4, 7-10, 23-24

You Will
Never Leave Me

My heart is glad and my tongue rejoices;
my body also will rest secure,
because You will not abandon me
to the realm of the dead,
nor will You let Your faithful one see decay.
You make known to me the path of life;
You will fill me with joy in Your presence,
with eternal pleasures at Your right hand.

PSALM 16:9-11

My Confidence
Is in You

You have been my hope, Sovereign LORD,
my confidence since my youth.
From birth I have relied on You;
You brought me forth from my mother's womb.
I will ever praise You.
You are my strong refuge.
My mouth is filled with Your praise,
declaring Your splendor all day long.

PSALM 71:5-8

On Holy Ground

So when the LORD saw that he turned aside to look, God called to him from the midst of the bush and said, "Moses, Moses!"

And he said, "Here I am."

Then He said, "Do not draw near this place. Take your sandals off your feet, for the place where you stand is holy ground." Moreover He said, "I am the God of your father—the God of Abraham, the God of Isaac, and the God of Jacob." And Moses hid his face, for he was afraid to look upon God.

EXODUS 3:4-6

Your Faithful Follower Praises You

All of Your works will thank You, LORD,
and Your faithful followers will praise You.
They will speak of the glory of Your kingdom;
they will give examples of Your power.
They will tell about Your mighty deeds
and about the majesty and glory of Your reign.
For Your kingdom is an everlasting kingdom.

PSALM 145:10-13

Lord, Remember Us

All kings on this earth
have heard Your promises, Lord,
and they will praise You.
You are so famous
that they will sing
about the things You have done.
Though You are above us all,
You care for humble people,
and You keep a close watch
on everyone.
You, Lord, will always
treat me with kindness.
Your love never fails.
You have made us what we are.
Don't give up on us now!

PSALM 138:4-6, 8

Bless the House of Your Servant

Your servant has found courage
to pray this prayer to You.
And now, O Lord GOD, You are God,
and Your words are true, and You
have promised this good thing to Your servant.
Now therefore may it please You
to bless the house of Your servant,
so that it may continue forever before You.
For You, O Lord GOD, have spoken,
and with Your blessing shall the house
of Your servant be blessed forever.

2 SAMUEL 7:27-29

May I Walk in Your Truth

$\mathcal{T}$each me Your way, O LORD,
that I may walk in Your truth;
unite my heart to fear Your name.
I give thanks to You, O Lord my God,
with my whole heart,
and I will glorify Your name forever.
For great is Your steadfast love toward me;
You have delivered my soul from the depths.

PSALM 86:11-13

Deliver Your People

LORD, I have heard of Your fame;
I stand in awe of Your deeds, LORD.
Repeat them in our day,
in our time make them known;
in wrath remember mercy.
You came out to deliver Your people,
to save Your anointed one.

HABAKKUK 3:2, 13

Hear Our Prayer for Forgiveness

O LORD, God of Israel, there is no God like You in all of heaven above or on the earth below. You keep Your covenant and show unfailing love to all who walk before You in wholehearted devotion. Listen to my prayer and my plea, O LORD my God. Hear the cry and the prayer that Your servant is making to You today. May You hear the humble and earnest requests from me and Your people. Yes, hear us from heaven where You live, and when You hear, forgive.

1 KINGS 8:23, 28, 30

May I Always Be Near You

One thing I ask from the LORD,
this only do I seek:
that I may dwell in the house of the LORD
all the days of my life,
to gaze on the beauty of the LORD
and to seek Him in His temple.
Hear my voice when I call, LORD;
be merciful to me and answer me.
My heart says of You, "Seek His face!"
Your face, LORD, I will seek.
Do not hide Your face from me,
do not turn Your servant away in anger;
You have been my helper.
Do not reject me or forsake me,
God my Savior.

PSALM 27:4, 7-9

There Is None Like You

*L*ORD, there is no one like You!
For You are great, and Your name is full of power.
Who would not fear You, O King of nations?
That title belongs to You alone!
Among all the wise people of the earth
and in all the kingdoms of the world,
there is no one like You.

JEREMIAH 10:6-7

Ezra in Prayer

At the evening sacrifice I arose from my fasting; and having torn my garment and my robe, I fell on my knees and spread out my hands to the LORD my God. And I said: "O my God, I am too ashamed and humiliated to lift up my face to You, my God; for our iniquities have risen higher than our heads, and our guilt has grown up to the heavens. And after all that has come upon us for our evil deeds and for our great guilt, since You our God have punished us less than our iniquities deserve, and have given us such deliverance as this, should we again break Your commandments? Would You not be angry with us until You had consumed us, so that there would be no remnant or survivor? O LORD God of Israel, You are righteous, for we are left as a remnant, as it is this day. Here we are before You, in our guilt, though no one can stand before You because of this!"

EZRA 9:5-6, 13-15

I Will Exult You

I will give thanks to the LORD with my whole heart;

I will recount all of Your wonderful deeds.

I will be glad and exult in You;

I will sing praise to Your name, O Most High.

When my enemies turn back,

they stumble and perish before Your presence.

For You have maintained my just cause;

You have sat on the throne, giving righteous judgment.

PSALM 9:1-4

You Are My Salvation

I will give You thanks, for You answered me;
You have become my salvation.
The stone the builders rejected
has become the cornerstone;
the LORD has done this,
and it is marvelous in our eyes.

PSALM 118:21-23

Deliver Me

On the day I called, You answered me;
my strength of soul You increased.
Though I walk in the midst of trouble,
You preserve my life;
You stretch out Your hand against
the wrath of my enemies,
and Your right hand delivers me.
The LORD will fulfill His purpose for me;
Your steadfast love, O LORD, endures forever.

PSALM 138:3, 7-8

You Are My Shield

You are my shield,
and You give me victory
and great honor.
I pray to You, and You answer
from Your sacred hill.
I sleep and wake up refreshed
because You, LORD,
protect me.

PSALM 3:3-5

You Are My Help

I prayed to the LORD, and He answered me.
He freed me from all my fears.
Those who look to Him for help will be radiant with joy;
no shadow of shame will darken their faces.
In my desperation I prayed, and the LORD listened;
He saved me from all my troubles.
For the angel of the LORD is a guard;
He surrounds and defends all who fear Him.

PSALM 34:4-7

The Lord Is for Me

*I*n my distress I prayed to the LORD,
and the LORD answered me and set me free.
The LORD is for me, so I will have no fear.
What can mere people do to me?
Yes, the LORD is for me; He will help me.
It is better to take refuge in the LORD
than to trust in people.

PSALM 118:5-8

In the Day of Trouble You Help Me

*Y*ou, O Lord, are good and forgiving,
abounding in steadfast love to all who call upon You.
Give ear, O LORD, to my prayer;
listen to my plea for grace.
In the day of my trouble I call upon You,
for You answer me.

PSALM 86:5-7

Teach Me Your Decrees

I gave an account of my ways and
You answered me; teach me Your decrees.
Cause me to understand the way of Your precepts,
that I may meditate on Your wonderful deeds.
My soul is weary with sorrow;
strengthen me according to Your word.

PSALM 119:26-28

Prayer of Isaiah

*B*ut we are all like an unclean thing,
and all our righteousnesses are like filthy rags;
we all fade as a leaf,
and our iniquities, like the wind,
have taken us away.
And there is no one who calls on Your name,
who stirs himself up to take hold of You;
for You have hidden Your face from us,
and have consumed us because of our iniquities.
But now, O LORD,
You are our Father;
we are the clay, and You our potter;
and all we are the work of Your hand.
Do not be furious, O LORD,
nor remember iniquity forever;
indeed, please look—we all are Your people!

ISAIAH 64:6-9

Lead Me and Teach Me

To You, O Lord, I lift up my soul.
O my God, in You I trust;
let me not be put to shame.
Make me to know Your ways, O Lord;
teach me Your paths.
Lead me in Your truth and teach me,
for You are the God of my salvation;
for You I wait all the day long.

PSALM 25:1-2, 4-5

You Redeem Me

For You are my rock and my fortress;
therefore, for Your name's sake,
lead me and guide me.
Pull me out of the net which
they have secretly laid for me,
for You are my strength.
Into Your hand I commit my spirit;
You have redeemed me, O LORD God of truth.

PSALM 31:3-5

Guide My Steps by Your Word

The teaching of Your word gives light,
so even the simple can understand.
Come and show me Your mercy,
as You do for all who love Your name.
Guide my steps by Your word,
so I will not be overcome by evil.
Look upon me with love;
teach me Your decrees.

PSALM 119:130, 132-133, 135

Send Me Your Light and Care

Send me Your light and Your faithful care,
let them lead me;
let them bring me to Your holy mountain,
to the place where You dwell.
Then I will go to the altar of God,
to God, my joy and my delight.
I will praise You with the lyre,
O God, my God.

PSALM 43:3-4

I Love Your Word

Oh, how I love Your law!
I meditate on it all day long.
Your commands are always with me
and make me wiser than my enemies.
I have more insight than all my teachers,
for I meditate on Your statutes.
I have more understanding than the elders,
for I obey Your precepts.

PSALM 119:97-100

Be Attentive to Our Prayers

*L*ORD, the God of heaven,
the great and awesome God,
who keeps His covenant of love
with those who love Him
and keep His commandments,
let Your ear be attentive and Your eyes open
to hear the prayer Your servant is praying
before You day and night.
They are Your servants and Your people,
whom You redeemed by Your great strength
and Your mighty hand.
Lord, let Your ear be attentive to the prayer
of this Your servant
and to the prayer of Your servants
who delight in revering Your name.
Give Your servant success today.

NEHEMIAH 1:5-6, 10-11

Forgive Our Sins

*L*ORD, if You really are pleased with me,
I pray that You will go with us.
It is true that these people
are sinful and rebellious,
but forgive our sin and let us be Your people.

EXODUS 34:9

Your Help Has Made Me Great

You make Your saving help my shield,
and Your right hand sustains me;
Your help has made me great.
You provide a broad path for my feet,
so that my ankles do not give way.
You armed me with strength for battle;
You humbled my adversaries before me.

PSALM 18:35-36, 39

Prayer of Daniel

Then Daniel blessed the God of heaven.
Daniel answered and said:
"Blessed be the name of God forever and ever,
to whom belong wisdom and might.
He changes times and seasons;
He removes kings and sets up kings;
He gives wisdom to the wise and
knowledge to those who have understanding;
He reveals deep and hidden things;
He knows what is in the darkness,
and the light dwells with Him.
To You, O God of my fathers,
I give thanks and praise,
for You have given me wisdom and might,
and have now made known to me
what we asked of You,
for You have made known to us the king's matter."

DANIEL 2:19-23

You Are Wonderful

*L*ORD, our Lord,
how majestic is Your name in all the earth!
You have set Your glory in the heavens.
When I consider Your heavens,
the work of Your fingers,
the moon and the stars,
which You have set in place,
what is mankind that You are mindful of them,
human beings that You care for them?
You have made them a little lower than the angels
and crowned them with glory and honor.
You made them rulers over the works of Your hands;
You put everything under their feet:
all flocks and herds,
and the animals of the wild,
the birds in the sky, and the fish in the sea,
all that swim the paths of the seas.
LORD, our Lord,
how majestic is Your name in all the earth!

PSALM 8:1, 3-9

Keep Me as the Apple of Your Eye

I call on You, my God, for You will answer me;
turn Your ear to me and hear my prayer.
Show me the wonders of Your great love,
You who save by Your right hand
those who take refuge in You from their foes.
Keep me as the apple of Your eye;
hide me in the shadow of Your wings.

PSALM 17:6-8

Wailing into Dancing

I will exalt You, Lord,
for You lifted me out of the depths
and did not let my enemies gloat over me.
Lord my God, I called to You for help,
and You healed me.
You turned my wailing into dancing;
You removed my sackcloth and clothed me with joy,
that my heart may sing Your praises and not be silent.
Lord my God, I will praise You forever.

PSALM 30:1-2, 11-12

May We Always Know Your Goodness

O LORD my God, You have performed
many wonders for us.
Your plans for us are too numerous to list.
You have no equal.
If I tried to recite all Your wonderful deeds,
I would never come to the end of them.
May all who search for You
be filled with joy and gladness in You.
May those who love Your salvation
repeatedly shout, "The LORD is great!"

PSALM 40:5, 16

With You There Is Forgiveness

Out of the depths I cry to You, LORD;
Lord, hear my voice.
Let Your ears be attentive
to my cry for mercy.
If You, LORD, kept a record of sins,
Lord, who could stand?
But with You there is forgiveness,
so that we can, with reverence, serve You.
I wait for the LORD, my whole being waits,
and in His word I put my hope.

PSALM 130:1-5

Help the Powerless

Lord, there is no one like You to help the powerless against the mighty. Help us, Lord our God, for we rely on You, and in Your name we have come against this vast army. Lord, You are our God; do not let mere mortals prevail against You.

2 CHRONICLES 14:11

I Repent in Dust and Ashes

I know that You can do all things;
no purpose of Yours can be thwarted.
You asked, "Who is this that obscures
My plans without knowledge?"
Surely I spoke of things I did not understand,
things too wonderful for me to know.
You said, "Listen now, and I will speak;
I will question you,
and you shall answer Me."
My ears had heard of You
but now my eyes have seen You.
Therefore I despise myself
and repent in dust and ashes.

JOB 42:2-6

Restore Us

*L*ORD, remember what has happened to us.
See how we have been disgraced!
Joy has left our hearts;
our dancing has turned to mourning.
The garlands have fallen from our heads.
Weep for us because we have sinned.
Our hearts are sick and weary,
and our eyes grow dim with tears.
But LORD, You remain the same forever!
Your throne continues from generation to generation.
Restore us, O LORD, and bring us back to You again!
Give us back the joys we once had!

LAMENTATIONS 5:1, 15-17, 19, 21

Prayer of Jonah

From inside the fish Jonah prayed to the LORD
his God. He said:
"In my distress I called to the LORD,
and He answered me.
From deep in the realm of the dead
I called for help, and You listened to my cry.
The engulfing waters threatened me,
the deep surrounded me;
seaweed was wrapped around my head.
To the roots of the mountains I sank down;
the earth beneath barred me in forever.
But You, LORD my God,
brought my life up from the pit.
When my life was ebbing away,
I remembered You, LORD, and my prayer rose
to You, to Your holy temple.
Those who cling to worthless idols
turn away from God's love for them.
But I, with shouts of grateful praise,
will sacrifice to You.
What I have vowed I will make good.
I will say, 'Salvation comes from the LORD.'"

JONAH 2:1-2, 5-9

Bless the Lord

Blessed be Your glorious name, and may it be exalted above all blessing and praise. You alone are the Lord. You made the heavens, even the highest heavens, and all their starry host, the earth and all that is on it, the seas and all that is in them. You give life to everything, and the multitudes of heaven worship You.

NEHEMIAH 9:5-6

Guide Me in Your Strength

*Y*our right hand, O LORD, has become glorious in power;
Your right hand, O LORD, has dashed the enemy in pieces.
And in the greatness of Your excellence
You have overthrown those who rose against You;
You sent forth Your wrath;
it consumed them like stubble.
You in Your mercy have led forth
the people whom You have redeemed;
You have guided them in Your strength
to Your holy habitation.
You will bring them in and plant them
in the mountain of Your inheritance,
in the place, O LORD, which You have made
for Your own dwelling,
the sanctuary, O Lord, which Your hands have established.

EXODUS 15:6-7, 13, 17

Do Not Forsake Us

*A*lthough our sins testify against us,
do something, LORD, for the sake of Your name.
For we have often rebelled;
we have sinned against You.
You are among us, LORD,
and we bear Your name;
do not forsake us!

JEREMIAH 14:7, 9

You Are My Deliverer

*H*asten, O God, to save me;
come quickly, Lord, to help me.
May those who want to take my life
be put to shame and confusion;
may all who desire my ruin
be turned back in disgrace.
May those who say to me, "Aha! Aha!"
turn back because of their shame.
But may all who seek You
rejoice and be glad in You;
may those who long for Your saving help always say,
"The Lord is great!"
But as for me, I am poor and needy;
come quickly to me, O God.
You are my help and my deliverer;
Lord, do not delay.

PSALM 70:1-5

You Light Up My Darkness

To the faithful You show Yourself faithful;
to those with integrity You show integrity.
To the pure You show Yourself pure,
but to the crooked You show Yourself shrewd.
You rescue the humble,
but Your eyes watch the proud and humiliate them.
O LORD, You are my lamp.
The LORD lights up my darkness.
In Your strength I can crush an army;
with my God I can scale any wall.

2 SAMUEL 22:26-30

I Seek Justice

O LORD of Heaven's Armies,
You make righteous judgments,
and You examine the deepest thoughts and secrets.
LORD, You always give me justice
when I bring a case before You.
So let me bring You this complaint:
Why are the wicked so prosperous?
Why are evil people so happy?
You have planted them,
and they have taken root and prospered.
Your name is on their lips,
but You are far from their hearts.
But as for me, LORD, You know my heart.
You see me and test my thoughts.

JEREMIAH 11:20, 12:1-3

You Are Near to Me

I cry out with my whole heart;
hear me, O Lord!
I will keep Your statutes.
I cry out to You;
save me, and I will keep Your testimonies.
I rise before the dawning of the morning,
and cry for help;
I hope in Your word.
My eyes are awake through the night watches,
that I may meditate on Your word.
Hear my voice according to Your lovingkindness;
O Lord, revive me according to Your justice.
They draw near who follow after wickedness;
they are far from Your law.
You are near, O Lord,
and all Your commandments are truth.
Concerning Your testimonies,
I have known of old that You have founded them forever.

PSALM 119:145-152

You Are My All

*Y*ou will light my lamp;
the L<small>ORD</small> my God will enlighten my darkness.
For by You I can run against a troop,
by my God I can leap over a wall.
As for God, His way is perfect;
the word of the L<small>ORD</small> is proven;
He is a shield to all who trust in Him.

PSALM 18:28-30

Prayers of Worship and Adoration

Suddenly a great company of the heavenly host appeared with the angel, praising God and saying, "Glory to God in the highest heaven, and on earth peace to those on whom His favor rests."

LUKE 2:13-14

The shepherds returned, glorifying and praising God for all the things they had heard and seen, which were just as they had been told.

LUKE 2:20

Guard My Life

*L*ook on my affliction and
my distress and take away all my sins.
Guard my life and rescue me;
do not let me be put to shame,
for I take refuge in You.
May integrity and uprightness protect me,
because my hope, LORD, is in You.

PSALM 25:18, 20-21

Your Unfailing Love Protects Me

I have talked about Your faithfulness
and saving power.
I have told everyone in the great assembly
of Your unfailing love and faithfulness.
Lord, don't hold back
Your tender mercies from me.
Let Your unfailing love and
faithfulness always protect me.

PSALM 40:10-11

You Alone Are God

For You are great and do marvelous deeds;
You alone are God.
Teach me Your way, LORD,
that I may rely on Your faithfulness;
give me an undivided heart,
that I may fear Your name.
You, Lord, are a compassionate and gracious God,
slow to anger, abounding in love and faithfulness.

PSALM 86:10-11, 15

How Priceless Is Your Love!

Your love, LORD, reaches to the heavens,
Your faithfulness to the skies.
Your righteousness is like the highest mountains,
Your justice like the great deep.
You, LORD, preserve both people and animals.
How priceless is Your unfailing love, O God!
People take refuge in the shadow of Your wings.

PSALM 36:5-7

Teach Me to Do Your Will

I desire to do Your will, my God;
Your law is within my heart.
I proclaim Your saving acts in the great assembly;
I do not seal my lips, Lord, as You know.
I do not hide Your righteousness in my heart;
I speak of Your faithfulness and Your saving help.

PSALM 40:8-10

You Are a Mighty God

The heavens praise Your wonders, Lord,
Your faithfulness too, in the assembly of the holy ones.
For who in the skies above can compare with the Lord?
Who is like You, Lord God Almighty?
You, Lord, are mighty,
and Your faithfulness surrounds You.

PSALM 89:5-6, 8

Bless Your People

$\mathcal{T}$he LORD bless you and keep you;
the LORD make His face to shine upon you
and be gracious to you;
the LORD lift up His countenance upon you
and give you peace.

NUMBERS 6:24-26

Be with Me, Lord

Oh, that You would bless me
and enlarge my territory!
Let Your hand be with me,
and keep me from harm
so that I will be free from pain.

1 CHRONICLES 4:10

The Prayer in Secret

"And when you pray, you must not be like the hypocrites. For they love to stand and pray in the synagogues and at the street corners, that they may be seen by others. Truly, I say to you, they have received their reward. But when you pray, go into your room and shut the door and pray to your Father who is in secret. And your Father who sees in secret will reward you."

MATTHEW 6:5-6

You Give Me All I Need

$\mathcal{T}$he eyes of all look to You,
and You give them their food in due season.
You open Your hand;
You satisfy the desire of every living thing.
The Lord is righteous in all His ways
and kind in all His works.

PSALM 145:15-17

Lead Me in Your Truth

Show me Your ways, O LORD;
teach me Your paths.
Lead me in Your truth and teach me,
for You are the God of my salvation;
on You I wait all the day.

PSALM 25:4-5

I Will Follow You

Your word is a lamp for my feet,
a light on my path.
I have taken an oath and confirmed it,
that I will follow Your righteous laws.
Preserve my life, Lord,
according to Your word.
Accept, Lord, the willing praise of my mouth,
and teach me Your laws.

PSALM 119:105-108

I Will Fear No Evil

*E*ven though I walk
through the darkest valley,
I will fear no evil,
for You are with me;
Your rod and Your staff,
they comfort me.
You prepare a table before me
in the presence of my enemies.
You anoint my head with oil;
my cup overflows.
Surely Your goodness and love will follow me
all the days of my life,
and I will dwell in the house of the Lord
forever.

PSALM 23:4-6

Comfort Me, Lord

All praise to God,
the Father of our Lord Jesus Christ.
God is our merciful Father
and the source of all comfort.
He comforts us in all our troubles
so that we can comfort others.
When they are troubled,
we will be able to give them
the same comfort God has given us.

2 CORINTHIANS 1:3-4

Create in Me a Pure Heart

Create in me a pure heart, O God,
and renew a steadfast spirit within me.
Do not cast me from Your presence
or take Your Holy Spirit from me.
Restore to me the joy of Your salvation
and grant me a willing spirit, to sustain me.

PSALM 51:10-12

I Trust in You

When I am afraid,
I will put my trust in You.
I praise God for what He has promised.
I trust in God, so why should I be afraid?
What can mere mortals do to me?

PSALM 56:3-4

In You I Find Shelter

Hear my cry, O God;
attend to my prayer.
From the end of the earth I will cry to You,
when my heart is overwhelmed;
lead me to the rock that is higher than I.
For You have been a shelter for me,
a strong tower from the enemy.

PSALM 61:1-3

The Prayer of the Pharisee and the Tax Collector

Then Jesus told this story to some who had great confidence in their own righteousness and scorned everyone else: "Two men went to the Temple to pray. One was a Pharisee, and the other was a despised tax collector. The Pharisee stood by himself and prayed this prayer: 'I thank You, God, that I am not like other people—cheaters, sinners, adulterers. I'm certainly not like that tax collector! I fast twice a week, and I give You a tenth of my income.'

But the tax collector stood at a distance and dared not even lift his eyes to heaven as he prayed. Instead, he beat his chest in sorrow, saying, 'O God, be merciful to me, for I am a sinner.' I tell you, this sinner, not the Pharisee, returned home justified before God. For those who exalt themselves will be humbled, and those who humble themselves will be exalted."

LUKE 18:9-14

To God Be
All the Glory

*W*orthy are You, our Lord and God,
to receive glory and honor and power,
for You created all things,
and by Your will they existed and were created.

REVELATION 4:11

Have Mercy

Sovereign LORD, do not destroy Your people,
Your own inheritance that You redeemed
by Your great power and brought out of Egypt
with a mighty hand.
Remember Your servants.
Overlook the stubbornness of this people,
their wickedness and their sin.
They are Your people, Your inheritance
that You brought out
by Your great power and Your outstretched arm.

DEUTERONOMY 9:26-27, 29

The Love of Christ

I pray that from His glorious, unlimited resources He will empower you with inner strength through His Spirit. Then Christ will make His home in your hearts as you trust in Him. Your roots will grow down into God's love and keep you strong. And may you have the power to understand, as all God's people should, how wide, how long, how high, and how deep His love is. May you experience the love of Christ, though it is too great to understand fully. Then you will be made complete with all the fullness of life and power that comes from God.

EPHESIANS 3:16-19

May Everyone Know You Are God

Lord God of Abraham, Isaac, and Israel,
let it be known this day that You
are God in Israel and I am Your servant,
and that I have done all these things at Your word.
Hear me, O Lord, hear me, that this people
may know that You are the Lord God,
and that You have turned their hearts
back to You again.

1 KINGS 18:36-37

You Are Our Provision

All creatures look to You
to give them their food at the proper time.
When You give it to them,
they gather it up;
when You open Your hand,
they are satisfied with good things.
When You send Your Spirit,
they are created,
and You renew the face of the ground.
May the glory of the LORD endure forever;
may the LORD rejoice in His works.

PSALM 104:27-28, 30-31

Let Your Promises Be Established

Lord, let the promise You have made
concerning Your servant
and his house be established forever.
Do as You promised, so that it will be established
and that Your name will be great forever.
Then people will say, "The Lord Almighty,
the God over Israel, is Israel's God!"
And the house of Your servant David
will be established before You.

1 CHRONICLES 17:23-24

You Are My Inheritance

Lord, You alone are my inheritance,
my cup of blessing.
You guard all that is mine.
The land You have given me is a pleasant land.
What a wonderful inheritance!
I will bless the Lord who guides me;
even at night my heart instructs me.
I know the Lord is always with me.
I will not be shaken, for He is right beside me.

PSALM 16:5-8

You Reign Forever

The LORD reigns forever;
He has established His throne for judgment.
The LORD is a refuge for the oppressed,
a stronghold in times of trouble.
Those who know Your name trust in You,
for You, LORD, have never forsaken those who seek You.

PSALM 9:7, 9-10

Jesus Prays for His Followers

"But now I am coming to You, and these things I speak in the world, that they may have My joy fulfilled in themselves. I have given them Your word, and the world has hated them because they are not of the world, just as I am not of the world. I do not ask that You take them out of the world, but that You keep them from the evil one. They are not of the world, just as I am not of the world. Sanctify them in the truth; Your word is truth. As You sent Me into the world, so I have sent them into the world. And for their sake I consecrate Myself, that they also may be sanctified in truth."

JOHN 17:13-19

Protect Me, Lord

You are my hiding place;
You protect me from trouble.
You surround me with songs of victory.
The LORD says, "I will guide you along
the best pathway for your life.
I will advise you and watch over you."
Many sorrows come to the wicked,
but unfailing love surrounds those who trust the LORD.

PSALM 32:7-8, 10

You Are My Strength

The LORD is my strength and my shield;
my heart trusts in Him, and He helps me.
My heart leaps for joy,
and with my song I praise Him.
The LORD is the strength of His people,
a fortress of salvation for His anointed one.
Save Your people and bless Your inheritance;
be their shepherd and carry them forever.

PSALM 28:7-9

I Delight in Your Word

When I discovered Your words, I devoured them.
They are my joy and my heart's delight,
for I bear Your name,
O Lord God of Heaven's Armies.

JEREMIAH 15:16

Great Is the Work of Your Hands

For You, O LORD, have made me glad by Your work;
at the works of Your hands I sing for joy.
How great are Your works, O LORD!
Your thoughts are very deep!
The stupid man cannot know;
the fool cannot understand this:
that though the wicked sprout like grass
and all evildoers flourish,
they are doomed to destruction forever;
but You, O LORD, are on high forever.

PSALM 92:4-8

Lord, Take My Troubles from Me

Listen to my prayer, O God.
Do not ignore my cry for help!
Please listen and answer me,
for I am overwhelmed by my troubles.
My enemies shout at me,
making loud and wicked threats.
They bring trouble on me
and angrily hunt me down.
My heart pounds in my chest.
Fear and trembling overwhelm me,
and I can't stop shaking.
Oh, that I had wings like a dove;
then I would fly away and rest!
I would fly far away
to the quiet of the wilderness.
How quickly I would escape –
far from this wild storm of hatred.
Confuse them, Lord, and frustrate their plans,
for I see violence and conflict in the city.

PSALM 55:1-9

We Love Your Law

*Y*our compassion, LORD, is great;
preserve my life according to Your laws.
Many are the foes who persecute me,
but I have not turned from Your statutes.
See how I love Your precepts;
preserve my life, LORD, in accordance with Your love.
All Your words are true;
all Your righteous laws are eternal.
Rulers persecute me without cause,
but my heart trembles at Your word.
I rejoice in Your promise
like one who finds great spoil.
I hate and detest falsehood
but I love Your law.
Seven times a day I praise You
for Your righteous laws.
Great peace have those who love Your law,
and nothing can make them stumble.

PSALM 119:156-157, 159-165

I Promise to Obey Your Word

*Y*ou are my portion, Lord;
I have promised to obey Your words.
I have sought Your face with all my heart;
be gracious to me according to Your promise.
I have considered my ways
and have turned my steps to Your statutes.
I will hasten and not delay
to obey Your commands.
Though the wicked bind me with ropes,
I will not forget Your law.
At midnight I rise to give You thanks
for Your righteous laws.
I am a friend to all who fear You,
to all who follow Your precepts.
The earth is filled with Your love, Lord;
teach me Your decrees.

PSALM 119:57-64

You Hold Me Up

If I say, "My foot slips,"
Your mercy, O Lord, will hold me up.
In the multitude of my anxieties within me,
Your comforts delight my soul.

But the Lord has been my defense,
And my God the rock of my refuge.
He has brought on them their own iniquity,
And shall cut them off in their own wickedness;
The Lord our God shall cut them off.

PSALM 94:18-19, 22-23

Saul's Dramatic Encounter

Then he fell to the ground, and heard a voice saying to him, "Saul, Saul, why are you persecuting Me?" And he said, "Who are You, Lord?"

Then the Lord said, "I am Jesus, whom you are persecuting. It is hard for you to kick against the goads."

So he, trembling and astonished, said, "Lord, what do You want me to do?"

Then the Lord said to him, "Arise and go into the city, and you will be told what you must do."

ACTS 9:4-6

You Make Me Dwell in Safety

$\mathcal{L}$ORD, lift up the light of Your countenance upon us.
You have put gladness in my heart,
more than in the season that their grain
and wine increased. I will both lie down in peace,
and sleep; for You alone, O LORD,
make me dwell in safety.

PSALM 4:6-8

You Give Me Peace

You will keep in perfect peace
all who trust in You,
all whose thoughts are fixed on You!
Lord, we show our trust in You by obeying Your laws;
our heart's desire is to glorify Your name.
In the night I search for You;
in the morning I earnestly seek You.
For only when You come to judge the earth
will people learn what is right.

ISAIAH 26:3, 8-9

You Freed Me

O LORD, I am Your servant;
yes, I am Your servant, born into Your household;
You have freed me from my chains.
I will offer You a sacrifice of thanksgiving
and call on the name of the LORD.

PSALM 116:16-17

Reveal Your Truth
to Your Children

"*I* thank You, Father, Lord of heaven and earth,
that You have hidden these things
from the wise and understanding
and revealed them to little children;
yes, Father, for such was Your gracious will."

MATTHEW 11:25-26

You Give Grace and Glory

O LORD God of Heaven's Armies, hear my prayer.
The LORD God is our sun and our shield.
He gives us grace and glory.
The LORD will withhold no good thing
from those who do what is right.

PSALM 84:8, 11

Acceptable in Your Sight

*L*et the words of my mouth
and the meditation of my heart
be acceptable in Your sight,
O LORD, my strength and my Redeemer.

PSALM 19:14

My Soul Yearns for You

*H*ow lovely is Your dwelling place,
Lord Almighty!
My soul yearns, even faints,
for the courts of the Lord;
my heart and my flesh cry out
for the living God.

PSALM 84:1-2

My Salvation Is in You

O LORD, I will praise You;
though You were angry with me,
Your anger is turned away, and You comfort me.
Behold, God is my salvation,
I will trust and not be afraid;
"For YAH, the LORD, is my strength and song;
He also has become my salvation."

ISAIAH 12:1-2

Bless Them, Lord

O LORD, hear me as I pray;
pay attention to my groaning.
Listen to my cry for help, my King and my God,
for I pray to no one but You.
Listen to my voice in the morning, LORD.
Each morning I bring my requests to You
and wait expectantly.
Let all who take refuge in You rejoice;
let them sing joyful praises forever.
Spread Your protection over them,
that all who love Your name may be filled with joy.
For You bless the godly, O LORD;
You surround them with Your shield of love.

PSALM 5:1-3, 11-12

You Made Me so Wonderfully Complex

Thank You for making me so wonderfully complex!
Your workmanship is marvelous – how well I know it.
You watched me as I was being formed in utter seclusion,
as I was woven together in the dark of the womb.
You saw me before I was born.
Every day of my life was recorded in Your book.
Every moment was laid out
before a single day had passed.
How precious are Your thoughts about me, O God.
They cannot be numbered!
I can't even count them;
they outnumber the grains of sand!
And when I wake up,
You are still with me!

PSALM 139:14-18

Index